# HELPING CHILDREN TO
# BUILD COMMUNICATION SKILLS

*Also part of the Helping Children to Build Wellbeing and Resilience series*

**Helping Children to Manage Anger**
Photocopiable Activity Booklet to Support Wellbeing and Resilience
*Deborah M. Plummer*
*Illustrated by Alice Harper*
ISBN 978 1 78775 863 6
eISBN 978 1 78775 864 3

**Helping Children to Manage Transitions**
Photocopiable Activity Booklet to Support Wellbeing and Resilience
*Deborah M. Plummer*
*Illustrated by Alice Harper*
ISBN 978 1 78775 861 2
eISBN 978 1 78775 862 9

**Helping Children to Manage Stress**
Photocopiable Activity Booklet to Support Wellbeing and Resilience
*Deborah M. Plummer*
*Illustrated by Alice Harper*
ISBN 978 1 78775 865 0
eISBN 978 1 78775 866 7

**Using Imagination, Mindful Play and Creative Thinking to Support Wellbeing and Resilience in Children**
*Deborah M. Plummer*
*Illustrated by Alice Harper*
eISBN 978 1 78775 867 4

**Helping Children to Manage Friendships**
Photocopiable Activity Booklet to Support Wellbeing and Resilience
*Deborah M. Plummer*
*Illustrated by Alice Harper*
ISBN 978 1 78775 868 1
eISBN 978 1 78775 869 8

**Helping Children to Build Self-Confidence**
Photocopiable Activity Booklet to Support Wellbeing and Resilience
*Deborah M. Plummer*
*Illustrated by Alice Harper*
ISBN 978 1 78775 872 8
eISBN 978 1 78775 873 5

# Helping Children *to* Build Communication Skills

Photocopiable Activity Booklet to Support
Wellbeing and Resilience

*Illustrations by Alice Harper*

**Jessica Kingsley Publishers**
London and Philadelphia

First published in Great Britain in 2022 by Jessica Kingsley Publishers
An imprint of Hodder & Stoughton Ltd
An Hachette Company

Some material was first published in
*Using Interactive Imagework with Children* [1998], *Self-Esteem Games
for Children* [2006], *Helping Children to Build Self-Esteem* [2007],
*Social Skills Games for Children* [2008], *Helping Children to Improve
Their Communication Skills* [2011], *Focusing and Calming Games
for Children* [2012] and *Inspiring and Creative Ideas for Working
with Children* [2016]. This edition first published in Great Britain
in 2022 by Jessica Kingsley Publishers.

1

A CIP catalogue record for this title is available from the
British Library and the Library of Congress

ISBN 978 1 78775 870 4
eISBN 978 1 78775 871 1

Printed and bound in Great Britain by Bell & Bain Limited

Jessica Kingsley Publishers' policy is to use papers that are natural,
renewable and recyclable products and made from wood grown
in sustainable forests. The logging and manufacturing processes
are expected to conform to the environmental regulations
of the country of origin.

Jessica Kingsley Publishers
Carmelite House
50 Victoria Embankment
London EC4Y 0DZ

www.jkp.com

# Contents

# Acknowledgements

I have collected or devised the games and activities in this series of books over a 30-year period of working first as a speech and language therapist with children and adults, and then as a lecturer and workshop facilitator. Some were contributed by children during their participation in therapy groups or by teachers and therapists during workshops and discussions. Thank you!

The suggestions for adaptations and the expansion activities have arisen from my experiences of running children's groups. Many of them combine elements of Image-Work (Dr Dina Glouberman), Personal Construct Psychology (see, for example, Peggy Dalton and Gavin Dunnett) and Solution-Focused Brief Therapy (Insoo Kim Berg and Steve de Shazer). Thank you to my teachers and mentors in these fields.

I have also found the following books helpful:

- Arnold, A. (1976) *The World Book of Children's Games*. London: Pan Books Ltd.
- Beswick, C. (2003) *The Little Book of Parachute Play*. London: Featherstone Education Ltd.
- Brandes, D. and Phillips, H. (1979) *Gamesters' Handbook: 140 Games for Teachers and Group Leaders*. London: Hutchinson.
- Dunn, O. (1978) *Let's Play Asian Children's Games*. Macmillan Southeast Asia in association with the Asian Cultural Centre for UNESCO.
- Liebmann, M. (2004) *Art Therapy for Groups: A Handbook of Themes and Exercises* (2nd edition). London and New York: Routledge.
- Masheder, M. (1989) *Let's Play Together*. London: Green Print.
- Neelands, J. (1990) *Structuring Drama Work: A Handbook of Available Forms in Theatre and Drama*. Cambridge: Cambridge University Press.

*Note: Please remember, if you are a parent or carer and you are concerned about ongoing and persistently high levels of anxiety or low mood in a child, it is always best to seek further support via your*

*child's school or your child's doctor. This book is not intended as a substitute for the professional help that may be needed when children are experiencing clinically recognized difficulties, such as chronic school phobia, severe social anxiety or childhood depression.*

*Wherever 'wellbeing' is used without further specification, this refers to social, psychological and emotional wellbeing.*

*As with any games involving the use of equipment, the parachute games outlined in this book should be supervised by an adult at all times.*

The following icons are used throughout to indicate the three elements of the IMPACT approach:

**Imagination**

**Mindful Play**

**Creative Thinking**

# Introduction

This book is one of a series based on the use of Imagination (I), Mindful Play (MP) and Creative Thinking (CT) to enhance social, psychological and emotional wellbeing and resilience in children. IMPACT activities and strategies encourage children to build life skills through carefully structured and supportive play experiences. Emphasis is given to the important role played by adult facilitators in creating a safe space in which children can share and explore feelings and difficulties and experiment with different ways of thinking and 'being'. This approach is explained in the accompanying eBook *Using Imagination, Mindful Play and Creative Thinking to Support Wellbeing and Resilience in Children*, which also contains many further ideas for games and activities and examples of how the IMPACT approach can enhance daily interactions with children.

## USING THIS BOOK

The games and activities in this book help children to:

- identify their current communication strengths and skills
- understand that their interactions reflect their beliefs about themselves and about others
- build and maintain a sense of enjoyment and effectiveness in the act of communication
- develop creativity in self-expression and recognize and celebrate the unique and diverse ways in which we each express who we are
- understand non-verbal aspects of communication.

### Facilitator involvement
All the games and activities in the Helping Children to Build Wellbeing and Resilience

series offer opportunities for facilitators to take an active part. Our participation reflects the nature of extended communities and gives us an opportunity to have fun alongside the children. Throughout the games and activities in this book, the term 'game coordinator' therefore refers to either adult or child participants, as appropriate for the level and stage of each group.

## Activities

The first section of games and activities, 'IMPACT Essentials for Building Communication Skills' (see section II), introduces children to the central features of the IMPACT approach – using imagery, being mindful and thinking creatively. There are also activities for group 'gelling' and for exploring relevant concepts such as self-respect and respect for others. Each book in this series has a different set of IMPACT essentials. With a slight change of emphasis, you will be able to use any of these to supplement your sessions if needed. You might also find it useful to add a selection of games and activities from two other titles in this series, *Helping Children to Manage Friendships* (which includes a variety of activities that could, for example, contribute to the development of active listening skills) and *Helping Children to Build Self-Confidence* (which includes activities for building confident communication in group situations).

The creative potential for supporting skill development is one of the wonderful features of childhood games. Play of this nature provides invaluable opportunities for children to learn through imitation, to experience the consequences of their actions and to experiment with different skills and different outcomes without fear of failure or being judged unfavourably by others. The multi-faceted nature of games means that in almost every game played there will be chances to enhance basic life skills, which, in turn, will help children to negotiate a variety of situations now and in the future. Because the activities in this book specifically focus on communication skills, there are no further suggestions for personal skills that might be developed or enhanced during play. However, examples of general/social learning have been noted.

Ideas are also suggested for adaptations. These illustrate some of the many ways in which a basic game can be simplified or made more complex. This also means that IMPACT games and activities can be revisited several times, thus expanding each child's experiences and offering opportunities for choice and flexibility in how they initiate and participate in social interactions. Naturally, all the suggested activities and strategies in this book should be considered in light of your own training and the developmental levels, strengths and learning differences of the children you work with. (See Chapter 12, 'Adapting Activities', in *Using Imagination, Mindful Play and Creative Thinking to Support Wellbeing and Resilience in Children*.)

There are many different non-competitive 'mini' games that can be used for choosing groups, coordinators (leaders) and order of play where appropriate. I have listed several options in *Using Imagination, Mindful Play and Creative Thinking to Support Wellbeing and Resilience in Children* (see Chapter 14, 'Group Structures for Playing IMPACT Games'). I suggest that the format is varied between sessions so that children can experiment with different ways of doing this. The choosing then becomes part of the social and personal learning.

### Reflection and discussion

Another important aspect of all the games and activities is the opportunity they provide for children to expand their thinking skills. To aid this process I have included suggestions for further reflection and discussion ('Talk about'). These consist of a mixture of possible prompt questions as well as suggestions for comments or explanations that can be useful when introducing or elaborating some of the ideas. (For more ideas about facilitating IMPACT discussions with children, see Chapter 11, 'Mindful Communication', and Chapter 13, 'Mindful Praise and Appreciation', in *Using Imagination, Mindful Play and Creative Thinking to Support Wellbeing and Resilience in Children*.) You may want to select just a couple of these or spread the discussion over several sessions.

During all discussions it is helpful to use language that reflects the assumption that children are already doing something (however small) that is contributing to the growth of their communication expertise. There are also several games which will naturally engender discussion during play and therefore do not include a separate 'Talk about' section.

### Expansion activities

Many of the games in this book are followed by one or more expansion activities. These are an important part of the process. They encourage children to recognize the benefits of a stepped approach to learning and to the process of change, and to understand how new skills can build on previous experiences, and how current skills can be strengthened.

### Activity sheets

Some of the expansion activities have accompanying activity sheets (see section IX). These are marked with icons representing imagination and creative thinking. Of course, creative thinking and imagination are interrelated. This in itself can be a useful discussion point with children.

I have found that children particularly like to draw or write about their imaginary world. Their drawings and jottings might then be the starting point for wellbeing stories.

(For ideas about how to create wellbeing stories see Chapter 17, 'Image-Making and Wellbeing Stories', and Chapter 18, 'Helping Children to Create Their Own Wellbeing Stories', in *Using Imagination, Mindful Play and Creative Thinking to Support Wellbeing and Resilience in Children*.) These can also be made into a personal 'Book of Wisdom' and perhaps act as reminders of some of the strategies that children might want to use again in the future.

Please keep in mind that IMPACT activity sheets are offered as supplementary material to expand and reinforce each child's learning experiences. They are not intended as stand-alone alternatives to the mindful play and supportive discussions that are central to the IMPACT approach.

# Exploring Communication Skills

## A MINDFUL PLAY PERSPECTIVE

The focus for this book is on confident and enjoyable self-expression for all children. The games and activities are a celebration of the skills that children develop in order to fulfil their communication potential. It is an acknowledgement of the power of language and the delight of words, of the wonderful instrument of communication that is our voice, the intricacies of muscle movement and coordination required for speech or for using sign language, the subtleties of facial expression and body movements involved in conveying the most complex of messages to others and the creative, imaginative ways in which we each express our thoughts and emotions. Above all, the games and activities in this book also offer a means by which children can explore the reciprocity involved in all types of communication and feel listened to, affirmed and valued. (See Chapter 6, 'A Child-Centred, Mindful Approach', Chapter 11, 'Mindful Communication', and Chapter 13, 'Mindful Praise and Appreciation', in the accompanying eBook *Using Imagination, Mindful Play and Creative Thinking to Support Wellbeing and Resilience in Children*.)

## MOTIVATION TO COMMUNICATE

Young children are motivated to engage in communication for many different reasons – because they want to convey information about the environment and about what they hear and see ('Look mummy, a train', 'I've just learned about the stars'), convey emotions and physical feelings ('I hate soup!', 'I feel sick'), ask a question ('How does this work?'), make a request ('Can I go to the park?'), explain ('It wasn't my fault. It just fell over!'), comment ('I'm building a big bridge', 'Jack is older than me'), refuse ('No! Don't want to!'), or answer a question ('I think it's in my school bag'). As they get older, communication becomes a means by which children define who they are. For example, they begin to share in communication with others in order to negotiate and cooperate, identify their successes and limitations, share and elaborate on feelings and thoughts, and formulate and refine their beliefs and values. For most children this is a natural progression. But there are always a multitude of variables that have the potential to disrupt the course of skill development or a child's confidence to use their skills appropriately.

As noted in Chapter 4, 'The Foundation Elements for Wellbeing', in the accompanying eBook in this series, *Using Imagination, Mindful Play and Creative Thinking to Support Wellbeing and Resilience in Children*, we can view wellbeing as being founded on eight different elements, one of which is *self-expression*. All eight elements are closely connected and interact with each other. Confident self-expression is, for example, partly dependent on a child's early relationships and how supportive and affirming these may or may not have been. This will influence how they view themselves in relation to peers and to other adults, such as teachers and support staff (foundation element *self and others*), and how they view their role in connecting with wider society or, for example, as an advocate for the natural world (foundation element *beyond self*).

Self-expression is also closely linked with *self-acceptance* and *self-confidence*, both of which are related to perceptions of self-efficacy (our belief in our ability to achieve something, such as managing a difficult conversation or giving a presentation).

The development of the foundation element of *self-reliance* affects how little or how much a child might be influenced by the opinions and evaluations of others, thereby also affecting a child's motivation to communicate their own opinions, strengths and challenges, or to engage in any communication that might be harshly judged. This, in turn, may affect a child's self-concept (linked with the foundation element of *self-knowledge*). And, while positive *self-awareness* is an important inner resource, children who do not have a healthy level of self-esteem can become acutely self-aware, perhaps becoming anxious about moments of natural social ineptness, and further withdrawing from any similar situations.

In other words, while helping children to develop their communication abilities and skills, we are also inevitably helping them to 'become themselves', and this will potentially have a profound effect on their long-term social, emotional and psychological wellbeing.

The complexity of these interactions illustrates an important point about how we might view communication skills. On the one hand, it seems counter-intuitive to reduce the complexity of the relational aspects of communication to a list of identifiable skills that we can become proficient at 'if we just try hard enough' – learning a set of skills does not necessarily make for an effective or enjoyable communication. On the other hand, knowing that they can build on their current skills and learn new skills that will enhance their interactions can be very empowering for a child.

The resolution to this seeming dilemma has to be in the ways in which a child's recognition, learning and use of communication skills is embedded in 'functional' communication, rather than being learned in isolation. In the IMPACT approach this relates to mindful structuring of games, activities and discussions so that children have the opportunity to develop and use their communication skills in a fun and natural way, interact with their peers and with adults without fear of being judged, and experience positive outcomes that are transferable to other contexts and are relevant to everyday outcomes – children can see the benefits of playing these games, and the learning will be immediately applicable in daily life.

What, then, are the skills that are central to confident communication? In my own work, I have found it useful to group these into the following six areas:

- Mindful attention: a child's ability to focus their attention internally to images, thoughts, emotions and sensations in a non-judgemental way, to focus mindfully on the outer world, and to have a sense of control over how and when they switch attention from one to the other. Mindful attention leads to effective listening – the ability to really hear what others are saying and to reflect on what is heard; and effective observation – the ability to observe and reflect on non-verbal aspects of interactions. (See Chapter 6, 'A Child-Centred, Mindful Approach', and Chapter 7, 'Helping Children to Be Mindful', in *Using Imagination, Mindful Play and Creative Thinking to Support Wellbeing and Resilience in Children*.)
- Imagination: the ability to imagine is an important feature of creativity and confidence in self-expression and of empathy and understanding of others. (See Chapter 8, 'Imagination and Images', and Chapter 9, 'Image-Making', in *Using Imagination, Mindful Play and Creative Thinking to Support Wellbeing and Resilience in Children*.)
- Understanding mutuality: the ability to understand the sharing that is involved in communication and the ability to cooperate and negotiate effectively. (See Chapter 3, 'Wellbeing and Healthy Self-Esteem', and Chapter 4, 'The Foundation Elements for Wellbeing', in *Using Imagination, Mindful Play and Creative Thinking to Support Wellbeing and Resilience in Children*.)
- Story-telling: the ability to sequence thoughts into a coherent 'story' that can be shared with others.

- Perseverance: the ability to keep going with difficult communication tasks and to overcome obstacles to effective communication.
- Adaptability: the ability to adapt to new situations and changes in communication contexts. Adaptability enables children to monitor and adjust communication in response to internal feedback ('This is going okay', 'I feel relaxed') and external feedback ('They look like they haven't understood what I mean', 'They're not really on my wavelength').

Within these ability groupings it is, of course, possible to be even more specific about the skills involved. For example, in relation to being able to cooperate and negotiate successfully in a verbal exchange any, or all, of the following specific skills may be utilized:

- initiating and ending an interaction
- asking/answering questions
- making requests
- taking turns in conversation
- giving personal information
- explaining/giving instructions
- using strategies for following complex instructions
- encouraging and reinforcing others
- keeping an interaction going/staying on the subject
- acknowledging the actions of others and giving/receiving feedback
- being appropriate and timely in interactions
- showing awareness of appropriate personal space (proximity to others)
- using appropriate problem-solving strategies in order to 'repair' interactions when needed
- being flexible in communication style (for example, according to the age or the relationship between participants).

As you can see, becoming proficient in so many skills would be a daunting task for children, but many of these skills will develop quite naturally within the context of IMPACT games and activities and the ensuing discussions. There will also be plenty of opportunities for children to reach their own insights and to develop their own ways of being creative in self-expression.

# IMPACT Essentials for Building Communication Skills

By doing the activities in this section you will be helping children to:

- think about different aspects of themselves, not just how they are dealing with any current difficulties
- identify their resources, strengths and skills
- see themselves as active participants in change
- begin to explore how the ability to imagine can be a helpful resource
- continue to develop or consolidate their skills in focusing and attending
- understand that what we think affects how we feel and behave.

# 1. Match up

Wellbeing focus:

☑ Self-expression

Examples of general/social learning:

☑ Being part of a group
☑ Building group cohesion
☑ Building trust

☑ Building self-respect and respect for others

As with other name games in this series of books, 'Match up' is a useful introductory game, but can also be played in a group where everyone already knows each other. The emphasis is on self-respect and respect for others. The adapted version also provides an opportunity to begin discussions about communication skills.

**How to play**

Players collaborate to make two sets of animal or object picture labels: one for players to wear and one to put in a bowl. Players pick a label from the bowl and find the matching picture worn by another group member. They then find out each other's names (each player will therefore meet up with at least two others). When everyone has found their matching picture, all the players return to sitting in a circle and take turns to introduce each other to the whole group.

**Adaptation**

• As a group, start by thinking of 10 communication skills such as listening, speaking to friends, explaining, sharing ideas. Players choose a skill from the list (or think of another skill) and make their own set of two cards naming something that they feel they do well – one to wear and one to put in the bowl. When they introduce each other to the group they affirm the skill: 'This is Tricia. Tricia is skilled at explaining things'; 'This is Izaak. Izaak is good at listening to others.'

**Talk about**

What did players need to know, or be able to do, in order to play this game? Can you think of a time when you have used these skills before?

Our names are a very important part of who we are. How can we show respect when we say someone's name?

How would you like to hear your name used in this group? Can you always tell what someone is feeling when they say your name? How can you tell?

Show the children how to finger spell their names so that they can introduce themselves silently to one other person or to the whole group. This could also lead to discussions about inclusion and about learning to sign.

# 2. Imagination castle

Wellbeing focus:

☑ Self-expression

Examples of general/social learning:

☑ Understanding empathy          ☑ Understanding different perspectives

**How to play**

The children sit or lie in a circle with their heads towards the middle and their feet pointing towards the outside of the circle. They are told that they are going to share an imaginary journey together to find an amazing castle or amazing museum.

Give the children the following instructions, leaving plenty of pauses to allow them time to explore the images. (For an example of encouraging feedback during imagery activities, see Chapter 9, 'Image-Making', in *Using Imagination, Mindful Play and Creative Thinking to Support Wellbeing and Resilience in Children*.)

When you are ready, settle yourself in a comfortable position and allow your eyes to close. Breathe slowly and fully three times – in through your nose and out through your mouth. Then forget about your breathing.

As your mind and body start to relax, begin to imagine that we are all standing on a path together. This path is going to lead us on a journey through the countryside to visit the amazing castle [or museum]. Start by having a look around you as you stand on the path. What can you see? What can you hear? Look down at your feet – what are you wearing? How does the path feel?

Now we are setting off along the path. What can you see now? Would anyone like to say what they can see? What can you hear? Touch something that is growing near the path. What can you feel?

And...just around the next corner of the path...there is the most magnificent castle that you could possibly imagine. It is so big that we cannot possibly see it all at once. We will need to explore it. Let's go...

Can anyone see how we get into the castle? Are there different ways to get in? Are there any other people here having a look around? Now we're inside let's go and see all the rooms. Off you go...tell us all what you can see and what it feels like to be in this castle.

(Allow the children a short while to explore.)

Now our exploring time has finished. We are all leaving the castle and walking back along the path. Wow! We will have such a lot to tell each other about what we saw and heard and felt in the castle.

When you are ready, open your eyes and stretch your arms and legs, give your hands a shake and then slowly sit up.

**Talk about**

In this game you used your imagination. What is the best thing about imagining somewhere that you have never been? How is this different to imagining somewhere that you know? Did you all imagine different things in the castle (or museum)? Did some of you 'see' the same things? Did you all have the same feelings about being in the castle (or museum) together? Why was this? Can you think of a way that you have used your imagination recently? How can being imaginative help us to share our ideas and feelings with other people? How can our imagination help us to understand other people's ideas and feelings?

## EXPANSION ACTIVITY 2.1. QUOTES

Set the children the task of finding some famous quotes about imagination. There are plenty of examples attributed to Einstein, for example, such as 'Your imagination is your preview of life's coming attractions'. Discuss the meanings of each quote and vote for a favourite 'quote for the day'.

## EXPANSION ACTIVITY 2.2. THE STORIES WE TELL (1)

Imagine what it would be like to be an ancient tree in a field or a new tree outside a house. What would you see and hear every day? What would be the best thing about being a tree? What would not be so good? What would you want to know about? Who could you ask? What stories would you be able to tell?

Make bark rubbings or leaf rubbings. Tear them into puppet shapes and make up a conversation between two trees.

## EXPANSION ACTIVITY 2.3. WISDOM RULES!

What sort of rules for visitors do you think the owners of a castle or museum might have? Why do you think they would have these rules?

What rules shall we have for this group?

Can you think of some rules that might be useful for talking in a group?

Can you think of another word for 'rules'? Is there a difference between rules, laws, suggestions and guidelines? If so, how do they differ?

Suggest to the children that they write a list of rules or guidelines for the group. Use this to start (or add to) their personal 'Book of Wisdom' or start a shared 'Book of Wisdom' for the whole group. The 'scroll' template (activity sheet 2.3) could be used for this.

# 3. Focusing and mindful breathing parachute game

Wellbeing focus:

☑ Self-expression

Examples of general/social learning:

☑ Building group cohesion     ☑ Building trust

**How to play**

Start by practising the mindful breathing activity (see Appendix A of the accompanying eBook *Using Imagination, Mindful Play and Creative Thinking to Support Wellbeing and Resilience in Children*). Then see if the whole group can focus on mindful breathing together, using a parachute to help them to coordinate this. Players stand in a circle. They hold the parachute at waist level and move slowly into the centre and out again, in rhythm with breathing in and out.

**Adaptations**

- If you don't have a parachute, the children could hold hands in a circle or hold a circle of rope or scarves tied together.
- Players say/sing different vowel sounds as they move the parachute up and down or move slowly in and out.
- Players increase/decrease their volume on a hum or a vowel as they move the parachute.

**Talk about**

What skills did you use in this game?

What happens when you focus on feeling your breath or moving slowly?

How easy or difficult is it for you to move your focus of attention from one thing to something else and then back again? Can you think of a time when this skill is useful? How would it be useful in a conversation, for example?

# 4. Skills

Wellbeing focus:

☑ Self-expression

Examples of general/social learning:

☑ Exploring self-efficacy          ☑ Building self-respect and respect for others

Building on a child's current strengths and skills is an important aspect of the IMPACT approach and features in other games throughout this series of books (see, for example, 'Exploratory activity 5.3. Skills and qualities' in the accompanying eBook *Using Imagination, Mindful Play and Creative Thinking to Support Wellbeing and Resilience in Children*).

**How to play**

The group divides into teams and takes 10 minutes to think of all the skills that are needed for making a cheese sandwich. They then come together to share their ideas and to produce a joint list. Can the teams come up with 20 or more skills? 20 would be excellent, 30 would be astounding!

When players have completed a joint list, choose a different task and see if any of the skills could be used for that task as well.

This game requires players to 'think outside the box'. Will they think to include such skills as weighing flour to make bread, or milking a cow in readiness for making cheese? Will they think of such things as the eye/hand coordination needed to cut the bread into slices or lay the cheese on the bread without missing it? What about patience? Following recipe instructions? Visualizing what you want the sandwich to look like? Being creative?

**Talk about**

When teams combined their lists of skills did anyone suddenly think of something extra to add? Why might this happen?

Think about the ways in which many skills are transferable to a variety of tasks and situations. Think about three skills identified in the game that would help you to give someone directions from your house to the local park or library, for example.

### EXPANSION ACTIVITY 4.1. MY SKILLS COLLECTION

The children use activity sheet 4.1 to list some of their current communication skills and skills that they are working on, or 'collecting'. They add these lists to their 'Book of Wisdom'.

# 5. Sharing feelings

Wellbeing focus:

☑ Self-expression

Examples of general/social learning:

☑ Building trust                    ☑ Building self-respect and respect
                                       for others

**How to play**

The game coordinator leads a very brief discussion about how different feelings could be thought of as different colours of the rainbow. For example, 'I'm feeling like the colour blue today because I feel calm'; 'I feel like the colour blue today because I feel sad'; 'I feel like the colour red because I feel full of energy'. Talk about the type of movement that might be used to show different colours of the rainbow. If you were feeling like the colour red, how would you move do you think? Would you move quickly or slowly? Would you be small and only move in a small space, or would you be big and move all over the room? Would the way you move feel heavy or light, or somewhere in between?

Ask the children what rainbow colour they are feeling today and why they chose that colour. Then the children feel what it is like to move around the room as their chosen colour.

**Adaptations**

- Everyone tries the same rainbow colour. Do the movements first and then ask what emotion/feeling the children had when they moved as this colour.
- Try three or four different rainbow colours in succession.
- Groups of children choose a rainbow colour to portray to the rest of the group, who then guess which colour/feeling it is.

**Talk about**

What colour of the rainbow is anger? What about excitement? Do anger and excitement have different rainbow colours according to the strength of the feeling?

Do all the blues move in the same way? How do different colours move?

Feelings can change very quickly, perhaps because of something that happens to us, or something that we see or hear. Is it easy to change from one 'mood' or feeling to another on purpose? When might that happen?

Because our moods change, this means that uncomfortable feelings, as well as nice feelings, will change, stop or fade away gradually. Sometimes it's hard to know why we are feeling a certain way. Noticing an uncomfortable feeling and telling someone about it can help us to cope with it.

## EXPANSION ACTIVITY 5.1. IMAGINING THAT FEELINGS ARE COLOURS

Complete activity sheet 5.1 in pairs or together as a whole group.

# How and Why We Communicate

By doing the activities in this section you will be helping children to:

- understand that we communicate with each other for many different reasons
- explore concepts of diversity and inclusion in relation to communication
- think about how we produce speech sounds
- experiment with intonation patterns and voice quality and how these can be altered to give emphasis or to convey different emotions.

# 6. Reasons to communicate parachute game

Wellbeing focus:

☑ Self-expression

Examples of general/social learning:

☑ Flexibility of thought        ☑ Understanding different perspectives

See '3. Focusing and mindful breathing (parachute game)' for some possible alternatives to using a parachute.

There is no 'Talk about' section for this game. Children are encouraged to discuss and negotiate throughout the period of play.

**How to play**

As a group, start by thinking of a variety of reasons why we might communicate with each other. Players stand in a circle and hold the parachute at waist level. The game coordinator says a word or phrase in a way that indicates one of the reasons (see the examples below and 'Motivation to communicate' in section I). This works best if the coordinator's intonations and facial expressions are overplayed. This can then also lead to discussions about different styles of communication, how we communicate emotions and the appropriateness of how we might express different levels of emotion in various situations.

Players try to move the parachute up and down to match the 'feel' of the word or phrase. For example, if the intention is to complain, then the movement might be fast and erratic. Once all players have agreed on how to move the parachute in unison, volunteers suggest other words or phrases that indicate the same intention. Players move the parachute while saying the new words or phrases. After two or three players have volunteered, the coordinator chooses another reason and a different word or phrase.

*Examples*

Wanting something: 'Please', 'Do you have?', 'Can I borrow?'

Describing: 'It's hot', 'It's very tall'

Remembering: 'A long time ago', 'When I was six', 'Last summer'

Reporting: 'My bike chain is broken', 'My watch has stopped'

Explaining: 'You can do it this way', 'The first step is'

Justifying: 'It was the right thing to do because'

Complaining: 'I hate this', 'This is not what I ordered'

Expressing emotion: 'I'm sad', 'I'm furious'

Describing an attribute/describing how I see myself: 'I'm a thoughtful person'

Negotiating: 'I'll try this if you can help me'

Denying: 'It wasn't me! I didn't break it!'

## Adaptation

• Players take turns to pick a reason and direct the rest of the group as to how they would like the parachute to be moved.

# 7. Guess who!

Wellbeing focus:

☑ Self-expression

Examples of general/social learning:

☑ Exploring self-concept          ☑ Dramatic awareness

### How to play
This works best in a fairly large group where the players know each other well.

A player is chosen as the first listener. They stand with their back to the other players. Three children take turns to disguise their voice and say a pre-chosen sentence, such as 'Hi, it's great to see you'. Player One must try to guess the speaker's real identity. They are only allowed one guess for each voice. If they cannot guess correctly, then the person who has managed to successfully disguise their voice takes over as listener. If they guess all three voices correctly, they choose the next person to be the listener.

### Adaptations

- Increase the number of guesses allowed.
- Give time at the start for everyone to practise their disguised voice.
- Increase or decrease the length of the spoken sentence.

### Talk about
Was it easy or difficult to disguise your voice? Why was this?

What makes voices sound different?

Have you ever 'lost' your voice? Why/when might this happen?

What did you do to disguise your voice? Can you change anything else about your voice (such as pitch, volume, accent)?

What do you like about your voice?

# 8. Shepherds and sheep

Wellbeing focus:

☑ Self-expression

Examples of general/social learning:

☑ Understanding links between feedback from others and self-monitoring

☑ Building trust

**How to play**

The children work together in pairs. One is the shepherd and the other is the sheep. The sheep wears a blindfold or covers their eyes. The shepherd steers the sheep into its pen (a square marked out with masking tape) by only using changes in pitch, for example humming with a rising pitch for 'go left', a falling pitch for 'go right' and a level pitch for 'straight ahead'. Once the sheep is safely in the pen the pairs swap over but start from a different position in the room, playground, etc.

**Adaptations**

- Use more subtle pitch changes for 'yes', 'nearly right', 'wrong way', etc.
- Steer the sheep to their pen using changes in volume or different vowel sounds.
- The sheep keep their eyes uncovered and are directed by non-verbal signals such as waving for 'go left' and standing on one leg for 'go right'.

**Talk about**

What skills did the shepherds and the sheep need for this game?

How many ways can you say the word 'no'? How does changing the pitch of your speech alter the meaning of the word?

What is sarcasm? How can you tell when someone is being sarcastic?

# 9. Name fame

Wellbeing focus:

☑ Self-expression

Examples of general/social learning:

☑ Exploring links between thoughts, feelings and actions

☑ Building self-respect and respect for others

### How to play

Players stand or sit in a circle. The game coordinator demonstrates a style of speech such as in the style of an adoring pop fan, a queen or king, a magician or a famous superhero. 'Over-play' the styles as much as possible! The children say their own names around the circle in this style. Repeat this with several different styles. Each player in turn then tells the group how they would like to hear their name. Everyone repeats the person's name in the chosen style at the same time.

### Adaptations

- Try varying different speech parameters, for example saying names very quietly, loudly, slowly, quickly, with a high pitch, low pitch or different combinations of these.
- Say names with different emotional emphases, for example grumpily, happily, sadly, courageously.

### Talk about

In what ways does your voice reflect how you feel? Think of someone you know who sounds very confident when they speak. How would you describe their voice?

# 10. Constructions

Wellbeing focus:

☑ Self-expression

Examples of general/social learning:

☑ Flexibility of thought

☑ Development of body awareness and positive body image

**How to play**

Challenge the children to research how we use our lungs for breathing and talking. Set them the task of constructing a model of the lungs from a variety of material such as bubble wrap, cardboard tubes, balloons, etc. Include some materials that probably won't be suitable. Invite the children to demonstrate their models and to talk about them.

**Talk about**

If you could improve the design of our lungs, what would you change?

What happens to our lungs when we talk? How does this compare to when we do physical exercise like running?

## EXPANSION ACTIVITY 10.1. ALL ABOUT HOW WE TALK

Set the children the task of finding out the names of the parts of our body that we use for talking (lips, tongue, palate, nose, larynx (voice box), vocal cords, lungs). Complete activity sheet 10.1 together.

# 11. Experiments

Wellbeing focus:

☑ Self-expression

Examples of general/social learning:

☑ Flexibility of thought          ☑ Willingness to experiment

**How to play**

Encourage the children to experiment with sounds and words. For example:

Try humming and then hold your nose mid-hum. What happens? Why do you think this happens?

Put the tips of three fingers gently on your Adam's apple. Now hum. What can you feel? Now say 'Sssssss'. What can you feel now? Why do you think this feels different?

Try saying 'moon' very slowly and feel how your throat vibrates. Then say 'spoon' very slowly. What happens?

Say 't' (tuh) and see if you can feel which part of your tongue touches the roof of your mouth. Now say 'k' (kuh). Which part touches now?

**Have fun with words**

Encourage the children to 'enjoy' words ('Who likes that word?', 'What is your favourite word today?').

Rename some natural elements using only two nouns (no adjectives). For example:

Clouds – rain baskets

Rain – water pearls

Garden ponds – life puddles.

Combine words to make new words (spoken or signed). For example:

Grecial – great and special

Kinful – kind and helpful

Rockle – rock and pebble.

Use the words in a sentence:

My best friend is really grecial; My holiday was grecially spectacular.

Thank you for being so kinful; Kinfulness is one of their best qualities.

That was a rockley decision!

Make up poems and stories using as many new words as you can.

# 12. My pet cat

Wellbeing focus:

☑ Self-expression

Examples of general/social learning:

☑ Understanding ambiguity          ☑ Flexibility of thought

This traditional speaking game (also known as 'The minister's cat') draws on knowledge of the alphabet and the use of adjectives but it could be adapted for any number of themes, such as verbs ('My pet cat likes acting') and adverbs ('My pet cat acts admirably'), food ('My pet cat likes apricots...') and so on.

## How to play

Players sit or stand in a circle. The first person starts off by saying 'My pet cat is an _____ cat (using an adjective beginning with 'a') and its name is _____ (giving it a name beginning with 'A'). The next player then does the same for 'b' and so on, to the end of the alphabet. Traditionally, when someone fails to think of a suitable adjective, they are out of the game, but this can, of course, be played in a non-competitive way too.

## Adaptation

- Describe the cat as belonging to a particular person, for example the shop-keeper's cat. Player A uses the alphabet – 'The alley cat is an acrobat' or 'The artist's cat is an awesome cat'. Player B says why – 'Because it can paint with its whiskers'. Players can choose to pass at any time.

# Effective Listening and Effective Observation

By doing the activities in this section you will be helping children to:

- understand the difference between hearing and listening and between seeing and observing
- think about strategies for listening and remembering and why listening is sometimes difficult
- think about why observation skills can be an important part of effective communication, and how the loss of one of our senses can cause another sense to be enhanced.

# 13. Sound detector

Wellbeing focus:

☑ Self-expression

Example of general/social learning:

☑ Adaptability

**How to play**

The game coordinator walks around the room making sounds on things or using objects (for example, flicking through a book, dropping a pencil on the floor). Players take turns to wear a blindfold and guess the objects being used.

**Adaptations**

- The whole group keeps their eyes closed and tries to guess the objects.
- Start with a general listening activity – what can you hear in the room? What can you hear outside the room? What's the closest sound you can hear?

**Talk about**

Is listening the same as hearing? When is it hard for you to listen? When is it easy? What sounds do you like to listen to? What sounds in the environment don't you like?

Is it easier for you to listen to sounds when you are wearing a blindfold, or is it harder? Why do you think that might be?

# 14. I remember

Wellbeing focus:

☑ Self-expression

Examples of general/social learning:

☑ Self-respect and respect for others         ☑ Understanding empathy

## How to play

In pairs, players take turns to talk about themselves for 30 seconds. Their partner then tries to remember everything they've heard and repeats it back to the speaker. For example:

I remember that you said...

I remember that you felt...

I remember that you went to...

The first speaker gives feedback on the accuracy of the information remembered. Pairs then meet up with one other pair and share the information about each other.

## Talk about

Did you use any strategies for listening and remembering? What worked? What didn't work?

What did you feel when your partner remembered what you had told them? What did you feel when they told someone else? When is it okay for something that you have said to be repeated to other people? When is it not okay?

## EXPANSION ACTIVITY 14.1. TALKING TIMES

Complete activity sheet 14.1 together.

It is helpful for children to understand that not only is it easier for us to talk about important things at certain times, but also that it is easier for others to listen at certain times.

Examples of easy and difficult times might be:

| It's easy when... | It's harder when... |
| --- | --- |
| Mum and I are having tea together | We are rushing to get to school |
| I'm happy/relaxed | I'm angry/tired/upset/very excited |
| The other person is listening well | Everyone is talking at the same time |
| I'm in a small group | I'm in a big group |
| I know everyone | I don't know everyone |

## EXPANSION ACTIVITY 14.2. LISTENING SKILLS

Use activity sheet 14.2 to encourage children to think about listening as a skill that requires focused attention. Talk about how we can sometimes hear several things at the same time (such as the TV, someone talking and the phone ringing), but we can choose which one to actually listen to.

# 15. Calling cards

Wellbeing focus:

☑ Self-expression

Example of general/social learning:

☑ Extending awareness

## How to play

Players select one card each from a pile of cards showing common objects that go together, such as a card showing a toothbrush and a card showing toothpaste, or a letter and a post box. Players stand in a circle and everyone calls out what is on their card at the same time. The aim is for each person to find their 'partner'.

## Adaptations

- Players find their opposite, for example up/down; big/little; hot/cold.
- Players find two others in the same category, for example happy, excited, elated.
- Half the group have cards with questions on such as 'Why is the girl laughing?' The other half of the group have 'because' cards, for example 'Because her friend has told her a funny joke'.

## Talk about

How easy or difficult was this game? Why do you think this? Did you have a strategy for trying to find your partner? What worked? What didn't work?

How do you know when someone has listened to what you have said? How do you show that you are listening? What sort of things do people say to show that they are listening? Is it easier or harder for you to listen/talk in a large group? Why is that?

# 16. Green space looking

Wellbeing focus:

☑ Self-expression

Example of general/social learning:

☑ Awareness of the wider environment

## How to play

Mark out a square in the woods, playground, garden or indoors. One child stands in the middle and looks all the way round, naming whatever they can see without moving from the spot. They then close their eyes and remember what was behind them, in front of them, under their feet, above their head, etc. in response to questions from other players.

## Adaptations

- Hang objects in the lower branches of a tree so that players have to really look to find them. Once they have found them all, they then close their eyes and try to recall them.
- Try to remember items on a shopping list by imagining them hanging on a tree.

## Talk about

What skills are needed for this game? How might these skills be helpful when we talk with each other?

What is the difference between looking, seeing and observing?

What strategies do you use to help you to remember things? How does the ability to remember help us when we are talking with friends?

# 17. I to eye

Wellbeing focus:

☑ Self-expression

Examples of general/social learning:

☑ Building trust                    ☑ Building group cohesion

## How to play

This is a surprisingly complex version of a warm-up or group gelling game that can cause great hilarity if played mindfully. Players sit or stand in a circle. The game coordinator starts the game by gaining eye contact with another player and then saying their own name.

The coordinator and the other player swap places silently. The second player then gains eye contact with a third player and says their own name before swapping places (in other words, they do not need to know the names of other players).

The game continues until every player has said their own name. As players get to know each other, the tendency is to say someone else's name instead of their own. In this instance it is up to the named person to stay still.

## EXPANSION ACTIVITY 17.1. LOOKING

Complete activity sheet 17.1 together.

Remind everyone that it may not always be appropriate for some children to use prolonged eye contact. Talk about what is acceptable for different families and cultures.

## EXPANSION ACTIVITY 17.2. KEEPING EYE CONTACT

Complete activity sheet 17.2. Ideas might include: talking for one minute on a chosen topic while trying to look at everyone in the group at least once; watching a video or TV programme and observing the level of eye contact for different speakers and listeners.

# 18. 'Eye' spy

Wellbeing focus:

☑ Self-expression

Example of general/social learning:

☑ Appreciating diversity

**How to play**

Players walk around the room and meet each other. Each time they meet up with someone they look at each other's eyes for at least 30 seconds, taking turns to describe exactly what the other person's eyes look like – not just the main colour, but as many other details as possible.

**Adaptation**

- Children use mirrors to draw their own eyes and colour them in with as much detail as they can. The group tries to guess the owners of the drawings.

**Talk about**

How easy or difficult was it to look into someone's eyes for 30 seconds?

Did you notice anything new about how our eyes are structured?

Look around the room. Can you see anything that you have never noticed before?

What do you like about your eyes? When you walk, where do you look? For example, do you look down at the ground or do you look around you?

How can eye contact help when we communicate with each other?

Who do you think does more 'looking' – the speaker or the listener? When you are listening, what do you feel if the speaker doesn't look at you?

# 19. Animal pause

Wellbeing focus:

☑ Self-expression

Example of general/social learning:

☑ Dramatic awareness

## How to play

It is night-time and all the animals in the zoo are prowling around outside their enclosures. Player One, the zookeeper, stands blindfolded in the middle of the room. When the zookeeper presses an imaginary 'pause' button all the animals stand still (so players need to keep watching the keeper).

The zookeeper points to one of the players and says 'Make the noise of a ___, (any animal). The one who is pointed at makes the noise. The zookeeper can ask the player to make the animal noise three times. If they are unable to guess who made the noise, they continue to be the zookeeper. If they guess correctly, they change places with that player.

## Adaptations

- The zookeeper is limited to two turns.
- Players all make noises of pre-chosen animals until the zookeeper shouts 'stop' and points to a player who is the only one who doesn't stop making their sound.

## Talk about

Why do we pause? Here are a few thoughts:

- To plan what we want to say.
- To give the other person time to absorb what we say.
- To think carefully before answering a question.
- To take a breath.
- Because we are filled with emotion.
- To emphasize a point.
- To keep a feeling of calmness.

# 20. Listening and observing

Wellbeing focus:

☑ Self-expression

Examples of general/social learning:

☑ Understanding links between feedback from others and self-monitoring

☑ Building self-respect and respect for others

### How to play

Players divide into groups of three. They are then given the following instructions (either verbally or as a written sheet):

> For this next activity you will take turns with two other people to each talk about something that you are interested in and that you think will interest your listeners. Each of you will have a turn at being speaker, listener and observer. When you are the listener think about the listening skills that we have already talked about. Your aim is to encourage the speaker and to try and understand what they are feeling. The observer's task is to watch and listen and give feedback to the listener on which skills they have seen or heard them use.

Remind everyone about what is acceptable as feedback. According to group abilities you could limit the feedback to 'One skill that I noticed you using'.

When everyone has had a turn in all three roles, players return to the main group and give positive feedback – 'Josh showed he was listening by asking a neat question'.

At the end of the group feedback, the facilitator also makes a positive comment about the way that players engaged with the game and praises the observers (that is, everyone!) for using such great observation and feedback skills. If there are any children who found this a particularly difficult activity, also praise the group for persevering or joining in or listening well, or comment on how you are noticing that everyone is doing well in thinking about focusing their attention. While praise needs to be genuine, it is important that children enjoy the activities and do not in any way feel judged for not getting it quite right (see Chapter 13, 'Mindful Praise and Appreciation', in the accompanying eBook *Using Imagination, Mindful Play and Creative Thinking to Support Wellbeing and Resilience in Children*).

# Understanding and Using Non-Verbal Communication

By doing the activities in this section you will be helping children to:

- identify different aspects of non-verbal communication and think about how these can enhance our ability to express how we feel
- think about the ways in which observing other people's body language can help us to understand how they might be feeling.

# 21. Hide and seek

Wellbeing focus:

☑ Self-expression

Example of general/social learning:

☑ Dramatic awareness

## How to play

One player leaves the room. The group throws a small soft ball or bean bag across the circle to each other until the player outside knocks on the door loudly three times before coming in. Whoever has the ball or bean bag at that point has to hide it quickly. The first player needs to look carefully at the facial expression and body language of all players to try and guess who has the object. Three guesses are allowed before a second player has a go.

## Adaptation

- A bead or a ring is threaded onto one long piece of string. The group hold the string lightly in their hands (palms facing downwards) and pass the ring around the circle until the player outside knocks on the door and comes in. All hands are then held at waist height so the person guessing can only go by facial expression or pure chance to find who is holding the ring.

## Talk about

What are the main facial expressions that everyone recognizes? Which part of the face is the most expressive part? Eyes? Mouth? Nose? Forehead?

# 22. If hands could talk

Wellbeing focus:

☑ Self-expression

Examples of general/social learning:

☑ Developing body awareness and positive body image

☑ Exploring links between thoughts, feelings and actions

Players need to stand in a large enough space so that they have room to move their arms and hands without touching anyone else.

**How to play**

The game coordinator instructs players to move their arms freely and at the same time to shake their hands, keeping them at shoulder level. When the game coordinator says 'freeze', everyone drops one hand and holds the other hand still in mid air. They then think about what name they would give to this 'frozen' gesture, for example 'inquisitive', 'ferocious', 'sad' or 'puzzled'. Each person changes their hand posture very slightly. What name would they give to this new gesture? Players invent a 'hand dance' changing from one gesture to the other and back again.

**Adaptations**

- Players try the same sequence of free movement, freezing and changing using their whole body and giving names to the different postures. Players invent a dance, moving from one posture to the other.
- Try the dances at different speeds and to different types of music.
- Players work together in pairs or threes to combine their dances.

**Talk about**

What happened during this game?

Even small changes in body language can make a big difference to how we feel and to how other people think we feel. Can you think of postures that look nearly the same but mean something very different?

We can show the same feeling in lots of different ways. For example, how do you show that you are excited? Some people may be very active when they are excited, some may use an 'excited' gesture like clapping their hands, and some may just smile or laugh.

Discuss the idea that we could show different emotions in almost the same way (for example, a child could cry because they're sad or because they're angry), and we need to look for other clues to help us to know what the feeling might be.

Act out different emotions and see if the children can guess how you are feeling. Talk about both obvious body language and more subtle things, like looking away.

# 23. Silent greetings

Wellbeing focus:

☑ Self-expression

Examples of general/social learning:

☑ Flexibility of thought
☑ Appreciating diversity

☑ Building self-respect and respect for others

This game requires plenty of space for players to move around freely.

## How to play

Everyone walks slowly around the room, silently greeting each other in a friendly way. For example, a little wave, a long slow wave, offering a 'high five', smiling, making eye contact, having a short 'conversation' between hands. The game coordinator may need to demonstrate a few ideas first. There should be no physical contact during this activity. The aim is to see how many different ways players can greet each other successfully.

## Adaptations

- Play a variety of music (such as culturally specific music, lively music, slow, gentle music) while players walk around the room and greet each other in ways that match the different rhythms and themes.
- Players meet and greet each other. After a short silent 'conversation' they say goodbye to each other non-verbally.

## Talk about

Did you learn a new greeting or get a new idea and then try it out with someone else? Did some ways of greeting seem easier than others? What was the most fun/natural/relaxed way to greet others? Which one felt most like 'you'? Did you change your greetings to match other people, or did pairs sometimes greet each other in completely different ways? How did that feel?

What are some of the signs that you could look out for to show you that people are thinking about you, or welcoming you into a group, even if they don't say anything (for example, 'thumbs up', a smile)? How might this help you if you are feeling anxious? Can you think of a time when you would be able to give this type of reassurance to someone else?

How close do we stand to the other person when we greet each other?

## EXPANSION ACTIVITY 23.1. BODY TALK

Sometimes even small movements or changes in body posture can show other people how we are feeling or can add extra emphasis to what we are saying. How many emotions can you show just by moving your shoulders? What about when you move your forehead/eyebrows?

**Let's imagine...**

Close your eyes and imagine someone that you know. What does this person look like when they are happy? How do they stand? Do you think they would be moving their hands, or would they be still? What would their face be like?

Make as clear a picture as possible in your mind.

Now imagine what this person would look like if they were nervous.

What about if they were sad?

How would they look if they were surprised?

When you are ready, draw or write about some of the 'body language' that you imagined this person using (activity sheet 23.1).

# 24. Keep it going

Wellbeing focus:

☑ Self-expression

Examples of general/social learning:

☑ Awareness of different perspectives

☑ Dramatic awareness

## How to play

Players sit or stand behind each other in a line. The first player taps the second player on the shoulder. This person turns to face the first player who then mimes a short sequence, such as planting a seed in a pot and watering it, or cutting a slice of bread and spreading butter on it. The second player has to remember the sequence to show to the third player, and so on. The final player tries to guess what the first player was actually miming.

## Adaptations

- The sequence can be made longer and more complicated or simplified to include just two parts.
- Players work in pairs and pass on sequences of gestures that involve two people cooperating, for example folding a large sheet together.

## Talk about

Did the sequence change as it was passed around the group? Why did this happen?

Do you use gestures when you talk? Why is it helpful to notice people's body language?

What does 'being on the same wave length' mean?

(If you watch good friends talking together, you will perhaps notice a very natural 'rhythm' to their conversation. It is not uncommon for people who are on each other's wave length to mirror each other's body movements. They will be talking at a similar volume and probably a similar speed. They are likely to be responding to what the other person is saying rather than introducing completely new topics.)

# 25. What's my line?

Wellbeing focus:

☑ Self-expression

Examples of general/social learning:

☑ Dramatic awareness          ☑ Appreciating diversity

**How to play**

Each child takes a turn at miming an occupation for the others to guess. The others in the group can ask 10 questions between them to help them to guess. Questions can only be answered by 'yes' or 'no'.

**Adaptations**

- As a group, make a list of common occupations before starting the game.
- Use pictures representing occupations for the child to choose from. These could all be kept in view so that the others can see they only have limited choices.
- Group members point to the picture representing the occupation being mimed.
- Play 'What's my game?', for example snakes and ladders, noughts and crosses.
- Pass around an imaginary hat. When anyone puts on this hat they can become a famous person or a character from a well-known story. They must then try to show who they are through mime. The rest of the group tries to guess who the wearer is pretending to be.

**Talk about**

What makes some occupations easier to mime than others?

What can a person's gestures/body language tell us about how they feel?

In what ways is miming different/the same as speech?

Why is miming useful? When might you need to use this skill?

Are there any words/types of word that are difficult to mime? Are there any that are impossible to mime?

# 26. Invisible pass the parcel

Wellbeing focus:

☑ Self-expression

Examples of general/social learning:

☑ Dramatic awareness          ☑ Flexibility of thought

**How to play**

The children are given a category to think about, such as 'Things you might find in a pencil case'. Everyone sits in a circle and passes an invisible parcel while the game coordinator plays some music. When the music stops the player who is holding the parcel pretends to unwrap it and takes out an invisible object from the chosen category, which they have to mime to the rest of the group. Everyone tries to guess the object. Play continues as soon as someone has guessed. If no one guesses, the parcel is passed around the group in the opposite direction.

**Adaptations**

- Use a real 'category' parcel with pictures in each layer of wrapping.
- As a group, think of a list of possible items first.
- Try miming different emotions at each layer.
- Throw and catch an imaginary object. Try and guess the qualities of the object as it is passed from one child to another. Is it big and heavy? Small and light? Spiky? Sticky? Smelly?

**Talk about**

Was it easy or difficult to think of items to mime? Why was this?

Did anyone mime an item that you were going to mime? How did that feel?

Was it easy or difficult to guess what people were miming? Why was this?

# Conversation Skills

By doing the activities in this section you will be helping children to:

- understand the basic structure of a conversation (beginning, middle and end)
- think about different types of question, when they would be used and what effect they can have on the speaker
- think about what it means to take turns in a conversation
- think about the skills needed for giving instructions and for giving a presentation, and how these types of communication are different to having a conversation.

# 27. Beginnings and endings

Wellbeing focus:

☑ Self-expression

Examples of general/social learning:

☑ Building respect for self and others

☑ Flexibility of thought

### How to play

Players sit in a circle and throw a bean bag or soft ball to each other. The catcher thinks of a phrase or question that could be used to start off an interaction, such as 'Did you stay for football practice last night?', 'Can I play too?' or 'I'm not sure how to do this. Can you help me please?' When everyone has had a turn, players think of ways to end an interaction, such as 'Bye. See you tomorrow' or 'Thanks for your help'.

### Adaptations

- If a player is unable to think of something, they can choose from two suggestions offered by the game coordinator or by the rest of the group.
- Work in pairs to devise a complete conversation of four sentences.
- The beginnings and endings are written on cards and placed in two piles. Pairs of players pick one from each pile. They have five minutes to prepare a conversation that makes use of the beginning and ending written on the cards. Pairs then demonstrate their conversation to the whole group.
- Pairs choose a card from each pile and must make up a spontaneous conversation using both cards within 60 seconds.

### Talk about

Do conversations always start with a question? Do conversations end with questions?

What happens if no one asks a question during a conversation?

Did pairs stay on the same topic for their conversation?

What helps you to stay on the topic?

What happens if one person in the conversation suddenly changes the topic?

What sort of things can you say to end a conversation? How do you know when a conversation is coming to an end? What might be some of the difficulties involved in bringing a conversation to a close? Think about face-to-face interactions and mobile phone/telephone conversations.

## EXPANSION ACTIVITY 27.1. CONVERSATIONS

Using activity sheet 27.1, talk about the wide variety of different types of conversation we can have – with one other person, in groups, about something serious, during play, about something familiar, about something new, and so on.

# 28. Duck, duck, goose

Wellbeing focus:

☑ Self-expression

Examples of general/social learning:

☑ Being part of a group

☑ Understanding the concept of inclusion

### How to play

In this well-known party game children sit or stand in a circle facing each other. One child is the fox. They walk slowly around the outside of the circle, tapping each player on the shoulder and saying 'duck'. When the fox taps a player and says 'goose', the fox and the goose run around the circle in opposite directions to see who can get back to the empty place first. The player left out of the circle then walks slowly around the outside and chooses another person. Play continues until everyone has had the chance to be a goose and a fox or until players are ready to stop!

### Adaptations

- The fox walks around the circle using different adjectives to describe the ducks, for example 'big duck', 'little duck', 'happy duck', 'sad duck', and the children listen out for a pre-chosen adjective to start running, for example 'quick duck'.
- Children listen for the 'odd one out'.
- Use characters from a story. The children listen out for their own name or for the name of one of the characters.
- Players hop in opposite directions to get to the available space.
- Mark the empty space with a picture so that the fox and the goose know where they are headed.

### Talk about

How easy or difficult was it for you to wait to be picked? Do you normally wait until someone says something to you before joining in with a conversation or a discussion in class? How is this similar/different to waiting your turn in a game?

How can you help others to join a group that you are already in?

What do you do when you want to join a group of people who are already playing or working together? What could you say to the group?

When is it easy to join a group? When might it be difficult?

# 29. Questions and answers

Wellbeing focus:

☑ Self-expression

Examples of general/social learning:

☑ Flexibility of thought          ☑ Understanding empathy

### How to play
Everyone in the group writes the name of a famous person on a piece of paper (or these could be prepared beforehand by the game coordinator). The papers are then shuffled and each person takes one without looking at it. This is taped to their back by the game coordinator. Players form a circle and take turns to stand in the middle, turning around slowly so that everyone can read the label. The player in the centre can ask up to 20 questions to find out the identity of the famous person. The other players can only answer 'yes' or 'no'.

### Adaptations

- Use animal pictures or characters from a book with which the players are all familiar.
- Allow more descriptive answers than just 'yes' or 'no'.
- Player One picks a card with a picture of an animal, plant, object or person on it. Everyone else in the group has 20 questions between them in which to guess what's on the card.

### Talk about
How easy or difficult was it to think up questions?

In this game you needed to listen to what was being asked and listen to the answers. How did you use the answers to each question to help you to decide on the next question?

Is it better to ask three questions all at once, or to ask them one at a time?

What type of question is likely to give you a limited amount of information? What type of question encourages people to give more detailed information? How does 'being interviewed' differ from having a conversation with someone?

## EXPANSION ACTIVITY 29.1. INTERVIEWS

Design an interview questionnaire together and ask each child either to interview one person in the group or to complete an interview as a 'do at home' activity. For example, they could ask questions such as 'How old are you?', 'What is your favourite TV programme?' and 'What do you like doing after school?'

## EXPANSION ACTIVITY 29.2. TAKING TURNS

Using activity sheet 29.2, talk about taking turns in conversations and asking questions to show a genuine interest in the other person. What do you feel when a friend asks you questions about yourself?

How do you encourage someone to carry on talking or to give you more details about something?

Relate your discussion to a variety of activities that require turn-taking if they are to work well. For example: team games, a joint story telling, board games, as well as conversations.

## EXPANSION ACTIVITY 29.3. KNOTS

Player One holds on to a ball of wide ribbon that is long enough to suit the size of the group. The end of the ribbon is passed around the group so that a complete circle is made. There is a knot in the ribbon. Any child can choose to speak when the knot reaches them.

## EXPANSION ACTIVITY 29.4. ROLE-PLAY

Demonstrate a conversation with another adult where turn-taking is not used and compare this to a conversation where you both take equal turns. Encourage children to role-play this in small groups.

# 30. Conversation drawings

Wellbeing focus:

☑ Self-expression

Examples of general/social learning:

☑ Coping with the unexpected      ☑ Flexibility of thought

**How to play**

Players work in pairs to construct a conversation through drawing, making marks and shapes with paint or crayons on the same piece of paper. Each player uses one colour and takes turns to draw their part of the conversation. Players must keep to their own half of the paper.

**Adaptations**

- Players construct 'happy' conversations.
- Players construct 'angry' conversations or 'I'm worried' conversations. Finish with a resolution and a calming down for these two interactions.
- Players work in groups of three.
- Two pairs of players construct their own conversation at opposite ends of a large piece of paper. After one or two minutes they then join up with each other to share a conversation between all four of them.
- Spread a roll of plain wallpaper across a large space (the school playground is ideal for this) so that players can move around and have 'art conversations' with as many different people as possible, joining groups, starting new groups or talking to just one other person at a time.

**Talk about**

What skills do you have that help you to join conversations and to start new conversations? What happens if people talk at the same time as each other? What happens if lots of people want to join the same conversation?

## EXPANSION ACTIVITY 30.1. LET'S IMAGINE TALKING SKILLS

This activity and 'Expansion activity 30.2' below both offer a chance for children to recap on what they have learned and discussed so far (use activity sheet 30.1).

## EXPANSION ACTIVITY 30.2. MIKE AND BILL

See activity sheets 30.2a and 30.2b. Use a role-play situation engineered between two adults if you think your group would pick out the important social skills, or lack of them, by watching and listening rather than from a story.

**Talk about**

Discuss the alternative, more successful scenario, demonstrating social skills if needed.

What could we do if we think someone has misunderstood us or we don't really understand what someone else has said?

## EXPANSION ACTIVITY 30.3. WHAT I LIKE ABOUT THE WAY I COMMUNICATE

Ask the children to remember a time when they have spoken confidently and had an enjoyable conversation with someone. Ask them to imagine being in that situation again and to ask themselves:

- What am I doing?
- What do I sound like?
- What does my body feel like?
- What am I thinking?
- What can I see?

Complete activity sheet 30.3 together. This is another opportunity for children to formulate a clear picture of successful communication skills. For example: I listened; I took turns; I asked questions; I looked confident; I felt relaxed; and so on.

# 31. Creative communications

Wellbeing focus:

☑ Self-expression

Example of general/social learning:

☑ Exploring links between self-
confidence and creativity

**How to play**

- Make sculptures and collages out of natural materials and then talk about them. Spend 10 minutes collecting items and give pairs of children 10 minutes to make their sculpture or collage. Then everyone looks at everyone else's work. Take photos so that you can talk about the experience later.
- Create a cake together. Making and sharing food can provide a very relaxed and natural way for children to communicate with each other and with adults.
- Invite the children to share their favourite poems and stories with the group. Then conduct a Question & Answer session in the same way that a director might answer questions at the first showing of their film.
- Make a story tent by draping a small parachute or large piece of cloth over a tabletop. The children learn a myth or legend and retell this to one or two other children in the tent.

(See also '6. Imagination tent' in *Helping Children to Manage Friendships*, another title in this series.)

# 32. Shadow puppet plays

Wellbeing focus:

☑ Self-expression

Examples of general/social learning:

☑ Dramatic awareness

☑ Exploring links between self-confidence and creativity

**How to play**

Each child makes a shadow puppet 'self' by tearing a piece of paper (tearing means that the shape has a 'fuzzy' outline and the children don't feel the need to make it look too realistic). Attach the puppet outline to a craft straw or a craft pipe cleaner. Use an overhead projector to project the shadow puppet on to a blank wall. Make up a shadow story about two or more children meeting for the first time.

**Adaptations**

- Cut out animal shadow puppets. Make up a story about the animals that meet each other in a zoo for the first time.
- Make hand shadows and have a conversation between, for example, a rooster and a rabbit. For ideas about shadow puppets, try The Bill Douglas Centre for the History of Cinema and Popular Culture at www.bdcmuseum. org.uk/kids/shadows-and-shadow-puppets or try one of the many books on hand shadows such as *The Art of Hand Shadows* by Albert Almoznino (Dover Publications Inc.).
- Make shadow puppet letters. Give the letters different characteristics and tell a story, for example '"Angry A" met "Calm C"'. What happened?

# 33. Instructors

Wellbeing focus:

☑ Self-expression

Examples of general/social learning:

☑ Understanding different
perspectives

☑ Understanding empathy

## How to play

Working in pairs, players take turns to explain to their partner how to draw an object such as a car, a tree or a house. The person who is drawing must follow the instructions as accurately as possible even if the end result doesn't look like the intended object. Players swap roles after a set time period.

## Adaptations

- Pairs sit opposite each other with a visual barrier between them (for example, a piece of card or an open book), so that they cannot see each other's drawings.
- The game coordinator provides simple line drawings for instructors to describe to their partners.

## Talk about

What could you do if you are uncertain about an instruction that you have been given? What helps you to give clear instructions?

How does giving instructions differ to having a conversation?

# 34. Criss-cross parachute game

Wellbeing focus:

☑ Self-expression

Example of general/social learning:

☑ Understanding concepts of joint
responsibility and encouraging
others

**How to play**

Players squat down, holding the edges of the parachute at ground level. The game coordinator says '1, 2, 3 parachute' or '1, 2, 3 sky high' and everyone stands up with arms above their heads to inflate the parachute. The coordinator then quickly gives an instruction for the children to cross beneath the parachute while it is still up in the air – for example, 'Everyone who had cereal for breakfast', 'Everyone who is wearing black shoes'. Players then take turns to give instructions (either volunteering or in turn around the circle).

**Adaptation**

- Players take turns to give instructions for moving the parachute in different ways at ground level (for example, like ripples on a pond, like great waves, like a sheet of ice) while two or more players walk across the surface in an appropriate way to match the motion. (See '21. Waves on the sea parachute game' in *Helping Children to Manage Anger*.)

**Talk about**

When might you need to give instructions to someone else? Have you ever needed to do this? If so, did you find it difficult or easy? Why was that?

# Sequencing Ideas, Telling Stories and Staying on the Topic

By doing the activities in this section you will be helping children to:

- explore skills of sequencing and telling cohesive stories about something that they have experienced
- explore the art of story-telling as a method of communicating ideas
- think about the skills involved in keeping to a topic.

# 35. Bean bag relay story

Wellbeing focus:

☑ Self-expression

Example of general/social learning:

☑ Understanding the concepts
of joint responsibility and
encouraging others

**How to play**

Players form a relay team. They retell a short sequence of events provided by the game coordinator, with each player telling one part before jumping to the next player, holding a bean bag between their feet. They then pass the bean bag to the next player without using their hands. When the last player reaches the finish line they say the full 'story' before throwing/dropping the bean bag into a large container.

**Adaptations**

- Lengthen or shorten the sequence according to ability and numbers of children in the group.
- Players make up their own story. It is up to the last person in the relay to bring the story to a conclusion.

**Talk about**

What helps you to remember a sequence of events?

What would make this game easier? What would make it harder?

**71**

# 36. 3-D noughts and crosses

Wellbeing focus:

☑ Self-expression

Example of general/social learning:

☑ Understanding the concepts
of joint responsibility and
encouraging others

## How to play

Draw out a large chalk grid of nine squares (3x3) on the playground or mark it out on the floor using masking tape. Place pictures of everyday objects, animals or plants in the grid. Mark three bags with a cross and three with a circle. Take turns to throw the bean bags onto the grid, trying to get three crosses or three circles in a row. Make up a sentence or a longer story together using the first set of three objects that are connected.

## Adaptations

- If a player's bean bag lands where another bean bag is, then the first bag is removed.
- If you are working with a group of six or more children, each child can hold their bean bag with the nought/cross clearly visible and jump into the squares instead of throwing the bean bag.
- Children throw three bean bags randomly onto the grid, and wherever they land fully in a square they name the objects and make up a story.

# 37. Skittle alley

Wellbeing focus:

☑ Self-expression

Examples of general/social learning:

☑ Exploring self-efficacy          ☑ Flexibility of thought

## How to play

Tape pictures or words onto play skittles or recycled plastic water bottles filled with a small amount of sand to make them stable. Players knock down three skittles with a bean bag or ball and then make up a question, statement or short story using these three words.

## Adaptations

- This very simple activity can be adapted for a variety of uses and abilities. For example, you could increase the number of skittles and move them further apart or closer.
- Use different coloured skittles for different parts of a sentence, for example blue for nouns and red for verbs. Tape words or pictures underneath the skittles. Players knock over one from each category and make up a sentence or short story using the revealed words.
- Players work in pairs or threes to knock down the skittles and construct a short story.

## Talk about

Stories have a beginning, a middle and an end. In what ways are stories like conversations? How are they different?

How can telling and listening to stories help us to understand and to describe how we are feeling? How can stories help us to understand how other people might be feeling?

# 38. Scrambled

Wellbeing focus:

☑ Self-expression

Example of general/social learning:

☑ Understanding the concept
of joint responsibility and
encouraging others

### How to play

Players work in teams. They are given a well-known story that they will be able to summarize in six easy sentences. They write these down or illustrate them in a simple way. They then scramble them up and present them for another team to sort them into the correct order.

### Adaptations

- Children invent their own story in six parts, scramble the parts, and see if an adult can unscramble them.
- Increase or decrease the number of parts.
- Retell simple sequences, such as making a cheese sandwich.
- Retell a sequence backwards.
- The children stand in a line or circle and say one sentence each of a well-known story. Mix everyone up and try to retell the story, still keeping it in the right order (the children need to remember which sentence comes next). Or tell it in the wrong order according to where the children are in the line/circle. One or more players try to reposition the children in the right order, moving them around and asking them to say their sentence as often as needed until the whole sequence makes sense (although it may not be the same as the original story!).
- Players retell something that happened to them recently, but in the wrong order. Where does the story start? Where is the middle? Where does it end?

**Talk about**

Was this an easy or a difficult thing to do? Why was that? Can a story be told in a different sequence and still make sense? Could you make a cheese sandwich in a different order? What might help you to remember and retell a sequence of events?

## EXPANSION ACTIVITY 38.1. THE STORIES WE TELL (2)

If you have not already done so, this would be a good opportunity to introduce the idea of wellbeing stories (see Chapter 17, 'Image-Making and Wellbeing Stories', and Chapter 18, 'Helping Children to Create Their Own Wellbeing Stories', in *Using Imagination, Mindful Play and Creative Thinking to Support Wellbeing and Resilience in Children*).

# 39. Just a minute

Wellbeing focus:

☑ Self-expression

Example of general/social learning:

☑ Understanding how individual behaviour affects others

**How to play**
In pairs the children take turns to carry on a conversation for one minute without straying off the topic and without repeating themselves.

**Adaptations**

- Speaker One talks for 30 seconds about a particular topic. Other members of the group can challenge if they think the speaker has changed the topic. If the challenge is agreed, the challenger then becomes the next speaker.
- Pairs have a one-minute conversation where Speaker One is trying to maintain the topic and Speaker Two is trying to change the topic.

**Talk about**
Was it easy or difficult for you to keep talking about the same topic? Why was this?

Compare talking about something you are enthusiastic about with something that you know very little about.

What are the differences between 'giving a talk' and 'having a conversation'?

Do you like to have pauses for thinking time when you have a conversation, or do you like to have fast conversations?

## EXPANSION ACTIVITY 39.1. SPEAKING IN A GROUP

Complete activity sheet 39.1 together. Compare and contrast groups of various sizes and who might be in each group. Do different children have different perspectives about groups?

Discuss what can be done to help the person who is talking (listen, sit still, keep good eye contact, smile, ask questions, etc.).

## EXPANSION ACTIVITY 39.2. WHAT I FEEL ABOUT SPEAKING IN A GROUP

Complete activity sheet 39.2 together. Talk about what helps and what hinders. Encourage the group to offer ideas and to help to problem-solve any identified difficulties. See also 'Confidence groups' in Chapter 13 in *Using Imagination, Mindful Play and Creative Thinking to Support Wellbeing and Resilience in Children*.

# 40. Story box trios

Wellbeing focus:

☑ Self-expression

Example of general/social learning:

☑ Flexibility of thought

### How to play
Collect miniatures or make objects from modelling clay/Play-Doh. Put three related items into a small box (covered sweet boxes or gift boxes are ideal). The children choose from a basket of boxes and make up a story about the three objects. The story can later be written up and displayed together with the box.

### Adaptations

- Distribute empty boxes to the children and ask them to choose three objects from a large basket of miniatures to put into their box. They then give this box to another child for them to make up a story.
- Children sit in groups of three and make up collaborative stories, taking one object each from the box.

### Talk about
Is it easier or harder for you to make up a story with objects or to make up a story with no prompts at all? Why is this?

Do all stories have a beginning, a middle and an end?

Could you use the same three objects that you had in your box to make up a completely different story? How many different story ideas can you think of using these three objects? For example, a sandal, a donkey and a straw hat could be used in a story about someone who goes on a donkey ride at the beach, a donkey that wants a straw hat but can only find discarded sandals, the adventures of a little boy who looks after the donkeys in a Spanish village, etc.

## EXPANSION ACTIVITY 40.1. THE STORIES WE TELL (3)

Choose a real event that can be retold as a story. Pick out three key words, objects or stages evident in this event. The children make up their own versions of the event using these three 'anchor points'.

# 41. Have fun with stories

Wellbeing focus:

☑ Self-expression

Example of general/social learning:

☑ Appreciating diversity

**How to play**

- Retell well-known stories from a different point of view.
- Share traditional stories from different cultures.
- Invite children and guest adults to tell a familiar story in different languages.
- Make a story chain: take turns to say one word of a poem or one sentence of a story.
- Use craft straws or craft pipe cleaners to make moveable figures. Make up a funny story based on the different movements that you can make the figure do. Tell your story to two other people.
- Tell stories about the funniest thing that has ever happened to you.

# 42. Surprise stories

Wellbeing focus:

☑ Self-expression

Examples of general/social learning:

☑ Flexibility of thought        ☑ Coping with the unexpected

**How to play**

A cloth bag full of interesting objects is passed around the group. The first player takes an object without looking inside the bag. They start off a story based on that object. The bag then passes to Player Two who takes an object and weaves that into the story as quickly as possible. The story continues until all objects have been used.

**Adaptations**

- Themed objects are placed in the bag, such as farm animals, a farmer and a tractor, or small objects that might be taken on holiday.
- Each player takes three objects and makes up a whole story within a strict time limit.
- Volunteers tell stories based on one or more objects from the bag.
- Player One starts off a story, then throws a ball of ribbon to someone else in the circle, keeping hold of one end. The catcher continues the story and holds on to the next piece of ribbon, throwing the main ball to someone else and so on, until the story is completed or the ribbon runs out.
- Based on the ubiquitous feely bag idea, a number of related items can be grouped together in a see-through bag. Players try to guess the theme of the bag, for example beach holiday, zoo, space travel. They then make up a story based on the identified theme.
- Players remove one object from a themed cloth bag and hide it under a box in front of them so that no one else sees what it is. They then describe the object to the rest of the group (this can also be played in pairs). Everyone tries to guess the theme from this one object. The bag is then passed to the

next person who does the same. Play continues until all the objects have been described, even if the players have guessed the theme.

**Talk about**

Discuss working in a group to deal with the unexpected.

What does it feel like when someone changes the story that you had in your mind?

Think about being spontaneous in conversations. It is often good to plan ahead, but sometimes we can over-plan things and get anxious about something long before it ever happens.

What sort of communication would we need to plan for? How might we plan for this (for example, a presentation). (See 'Exploratory activity 9.4. Taking steps' and the example of Andrew and Marcus in Chapter 9 in *Using Imagination, Mindful Play and Creative Thinking to Support Wellbeing and Resilience in Children*.)

# Celebrating Together

These activities provide an opportunity for recapping and celebrating. There are therefore no suggestions for general/social learning.

You might also give time for children to vote for a favourite story to be told or a favourite game to play – just for fun!

# 43. Communication channels

Wellbeing focus:

☑ Self-expression

**How to play**
Just for fun!

Players divide into teams. Each team uses art materials and masking tape to make something that they could use to send messages to outer space (set a time limit of 10 minutes).

Teams then demonstrate the use of their remarkable communication equipment!

**Adaptation**

* Combine everybody's structures and make a giant communication system.

### EXPANSION ACTIVITY 43.1. CONTACT

Read activity sheet 43.1 together and share ideas about possible questions.

# 44. Celebrating

Wellbeing focus:

☑ Self-expression

## How to play

Create a wooden totem pole with hooks and platforms that can be used for hanging objects on. What communication strengths/skills/qualities do the children have? How might these be represented on a totem pole? The children find or make objects to put on the totem pole and celebrate their achievements.

## Adaptations

- Make mini totem poles out of kitchen paper roll holders or the cardboard centres of kitchen paper rolls. Paint them with bright colours and use drawing pins or glue to attach small objects and pictures.
- Make clay totem poles with animals and plants to represent personal qualities or personal achievements.

# Activity Sheets

The activity sheets in this section can be adapted for discussion or used as a basis for devising more complex activity sheets for older children.

Where possible, I suggest that you encourage children to draw rather than to write, and to work together rather than to sit quietly completing activity sheets on their own. This sharing and talking will not only help to foster collaborative, mutually respectful relationships; it also offers an opportunity for each child to enrich their understanding of the benefits of using imagery, being mindful and thinking creatively.

## ACTIVITY SHEET 2.3. WISDOM RULES!

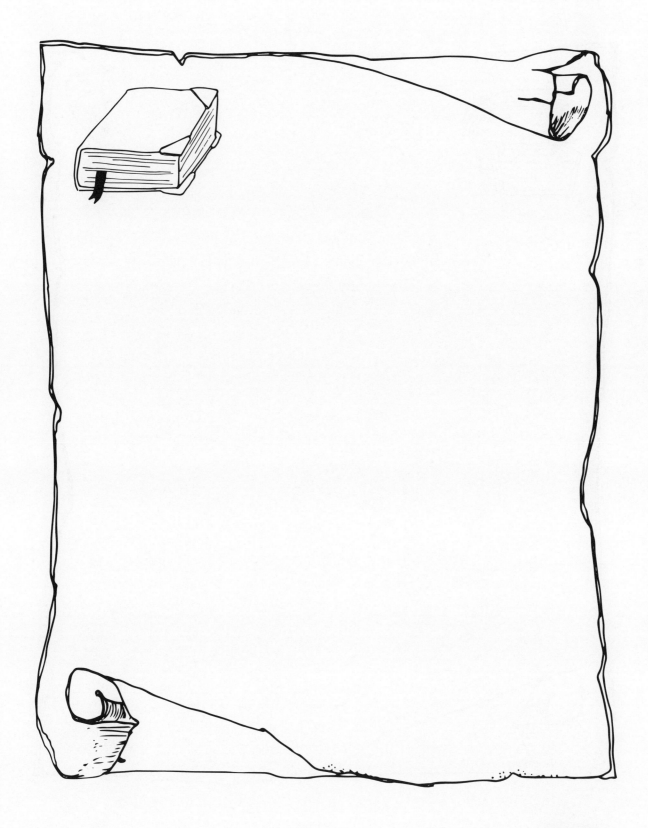

## ACTIVITY SHEET 4.1. MY SKILLS COLLECTION

Fill the scroll with drawings or words to show some of the skills that you already have and some that you are starting to collect.

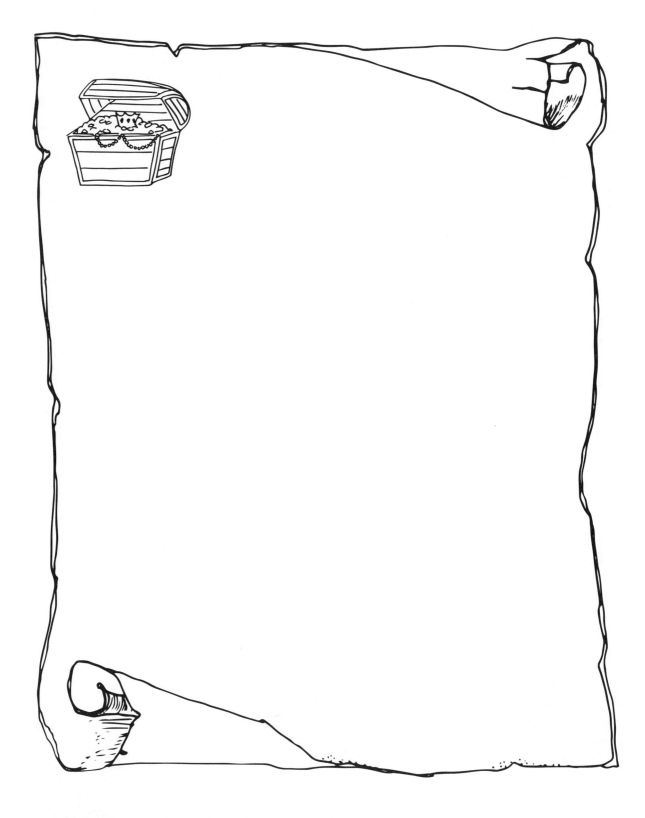

## ACTIVITY SHEET 5.1. IMAGINING THAT FEELINGS ARE COLOURS

Alexi and Agata are best friends.

They both like to use their imagination. Sometimes they use their imaginations to help them to describe how they are feeling.

Today, Alexi told Agata that if they described their feelings as a rainbow colour then they would choose the colour red because they feel very brave and strong.

Agata said that yesterday they would have felt red too because they felt energetic, but today they would feel blue because they feel very calm.

Which rainbow colour would you use to describe how you feel today?

Today I feel like the rainbow colour...

......................................................................................................

Because...

......................................................................................................

......................................................................................................

......................................................................................................

......................................................................................................

......................................................................................................

......................................................................................................

Draw or write about the rainbow colour that you have chosen.

Now you are really giving your imagination a good work out!

## ACTIVITY SHEET 10.1. ALL ABOUT HOW WE TALK

When you talk, you use different parts of your mouth and throat to make speech sounds. Sounds go together to make words and words can go together to make sentences.

Everyone sounds different when they talk because we all have different shaped mouths and throats and we move our speech muscles in slightly different ways. See if you can find out the names of some of the parts of the body that we use when we talk. Draw or write about them here.

## ACTIVITY SHEET 14.1. TALKING TIMES

Are there times when you feel that it's difficult for you to say what you want to say? Let's think of some times when it's easy to talk to each other and some times when it's not so easy.

It's easy to talk when...

...........................................................................................................

...........................................................................................................

...........................................................................................................

...........................................................................................................

...........................................................................................................

...........................................................................................................

It's harder to talk when...

...........................................................................................................

...........................................................................................................

...........................................................................................................

...........................................................................................................

...........................................................................................................

...........................................................................................................

## ACTIVITY SHEET 14.2. LISTENING SKILLS

Do you think that listening is the same as hearing?

Imagine that you are walking in a busy town with someone in your family. Draw or write all the things that you imagine yourself hearing.

Now put a circle around the things you would actually listen to. Can you listen to more than one thing at the same time?

## ACTIVITY SHEET 17.1. LOOKING

Why is it helpful to look at each other when we are talking?

....................................................................................................

....................................................................................................

....................................................................................................

....................................................................................................

Who does the most looking? Is it the person who is speaking or the person who is listening?

....................................................................................................

....................................................................................................

....................................................................................................

....................................................................................................

Imagine what it feels like when the person you are talking to isn't looking at you.

....................................................................................................

....................................................................................................

....................................................................................................

....................................................................................................

Imagine that you are talking to your friends and you are looking down at the floor. Imagine what your friends might be thinking.

....................................................................................................

....................................................................................................

....................................................................................................

....................................................................................................

## ACTIVITY SHEET 17.2. KEEPING EYE CONTACT

If people are able to look at each other easily when they are talking and listening, this is called 'keeping eye contact'.

Lots of people find this very difficult to do, especially if they are feeling a bit shy.

Keeping just the right amount of eye contact is an important part of feeling and looking confident. So now you're going to put your imagination to work by thinking up some games for practising eye contact.

Draw or write about your games here.

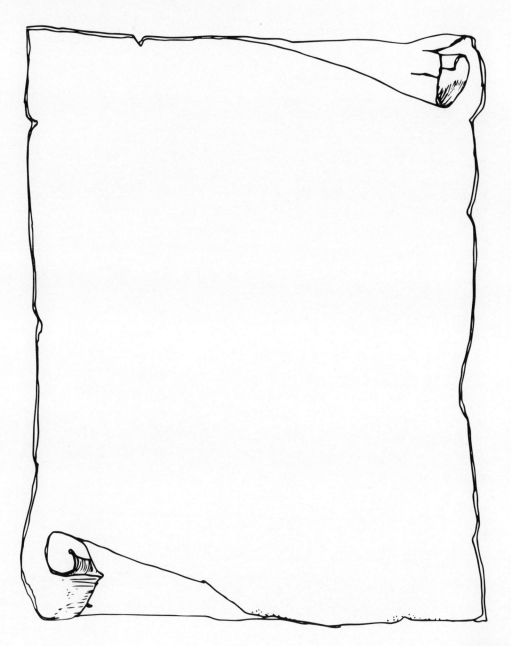

## ACTIVITY SHEET 23.1. BODY TALK

Draw or write about what you imagined when you thought about someone's body language.

## ACTIVITY SHEET 27.1. CONVERSATIONS

What does the word 'conversation' mean?

Draw a picture or write about a conversation you have had today. Who were you talking with? Who started the conversation? What was the conversation about? Who did the most talking? Who did the most listening? How did the conversation end?

## ACTIVITY SHEET 29.2. TAKING TURNS

What do we mean when we talk about 'taking turns'?

.......................................................................................

.......................................................................................

Why is it important to take turns when we talk to each other?

.......................................................................................

.......................................................................................

What would happen if we didn't take turns when we talked to each other? Imagine yourself having a conversation with some friends. Imagine that they are talking so much that you don't get a chance to say anything. What do you feel? What happens? What would you like to do? Draw or write about what happens here.

## ACTIVITY SHEET 30.1. LET'S IMAGINE TALKING SKILLS

Imagine that you are watching TV. You are watching a programme about the two friends, Simon and Jenny. They are having a conversation about the day they went on a school trip together. What are they doing when they talk to each other? Where are they looking? How do they sound? Do they both talk at the same time?

See if you can fill the speech bubble with lots of words to describe helpful talking skills.

## ACTIVITY SHEET 30.2A. MIKE AND BILL

See if you can spot all the mistakes that Mike makes in this story.

One day Mike was mending his skateboard outside his house when Bill walked by. Mike heard Bill's footsteps and looked up. Bill waved and said 'Hi Mike!' Mike looked back at his skateboard and carried on trying to fix the wheel.

'What are you doing?' asked Bill, kneeling down beside Mike.

'My dad gave it to me,' said Mike. 'I think he's at work.'

'It's a great looking skateboard,' said Bill. 'How did the wheel come off?'

Mike didn't answer, so Bill carried on talking.

'I used to have a skateboard but it broke when my brother tried to race it down a steep hill and it crashed into a tree at the bottom. I was really fed up and...'

'Sally isn't at home, so that means we can have fish pie for tea,' Mike said suddenly.

Bill pulled a face. He wrinkled his nose and curled his lips as though he'd tasted something really disgusting. 'Oh I love fish pie,' he said.

'Do you?' asked Mike, not looking up.

'No 'course not...can't stand it,' replied Bill. 'And anyway, what's fish pie got to do with Sally?'

But Mike had fixed the wheel on his skateboard and was ready to try it out. 'Bye then,' called Bill. 'See you at school tomorrow.'

'I wonder if Bill's got that new computer game yet,' thought Mike as he raced down the path on his board.

## ACTIVITY SHEET 30.2B. MIKE AND BILL

How many mistakes did you spot? Write them here.

## ACTIVITY SHEET 30.3. WHAT I LIKE ABOUT THE WAY I COMMUNICATE

Think about your own talking now. Think about all the things that you do when you talk.

Imagine that you have just had a long conversation with a friend. Write a list of all the things that you did to help the conversation to go well.

I imagined that I was talking to _____

This is what I did to help the conversation to go well:

## ACTIVITY SHEET 39.1. SPEAKING IN A GROUP

Talking to just one person sometimes feels different from talking in a group.

Let's think about this a bit more.

### Let's imagine...

Imagine that you are with some friends and you are telling them about something that you did yesterday. Where do you imagine yourself being? How do you feel?

Now imagine giving a talk to your whole class. Does that feel different or the same?

Imagine that your talk has finished and it went really well. What did your classmates do that helped it to go well? What did you do? Write or draw about some of the feelings.

## ACTIVITY SHEET 39.2. WHAT I FEEL ABOUT SPEAKING IN A GROUP

If I was going to speak in a group it would be okay if...

It would be difficult for me if...

## ACTIVITY SHEET 43.1. CONTACT

Let's imagine that you have contacted a creature from outer space with your communication system. Think of three things that you would want to ask.

..................................................................................

..................................................................................

..................................................................................

Now imagine that you are from outer space. You don't know anything about Earth or the people who live here. See if you can think of three things that you would ask.

..................................................................................

..................................................................................

..................................................................................

Draw your communication system for sending messages to outer space.

## HELPING CHILDREN TO MANAGE ANGER

Photocopiable Activity Booklet to Support Wellbeing and Resilience
*Deborah M. Plummer*

£14.99 | $19.95 | PB | 112PP | ISBN 978 1 78775 863 6 | EISBN 978 1 78775 864 3

Anger is a very difficult and often misunderstood emotion for children to experience. Facilitating the healthy management of this natural but challenging emotion is crucial for social, psychological and emotional wellbeing and resilience in children. This book provides varied and straightforward activities for teachers, parents and therapists to creatively engage with children and help them manage anger. It allows space to explore anger and varying degrees of emotion whilst providing help on how to manage them, allowing children to have better and healthier emotional self-awareness.

The accompanying ebook *Using Imagination, Mindful Play and Creative Thinking to Support Wellbeing and Resilience in Children* describes the theory behind this approach and gives examples and guidance for using the activities.

## HELPING CHILDREN TO MANAGE TRANSITIONS

Photocopiable Activity Booklet to Support Wellbeing and Resilience
*Deborah M. Plummer*

£14.99 | $19.95 | PB | 112PP | ISBN 978 1 78775 861 2 | EISBN 978 1 78775 862 9

Change and transitions are inevitable but can be an overwhelming and intimidating time for children. Facilitating the healthy management of transitions is crucial for social, psychological and emotional wellbeing and resilience in children. This book provides varied and straightforward activities for teachers, parents and therapists to creatively engage with children and help them process and manage transitions. It aids children in identifying their worries and fears about transitions and facilitates them in building skills and strategies that help them to cope during times of change. It also encourages children to explore the potential benefits and enjoyment that can sometimes be a result of change.

The accompanying ebook *Using Imagination, Mindful Play and Creative Thinking to Support Wellbeing and Resilience in Children* describes the theory behind this approach and gives examples and guidance for using the activities.

## HELPING CHILDREN TO MANAGE STRESS

Photocopiable Activity Booklet to Support Wellbeing and Resilience
*Deborah M. Plummer*

£14.99 | $19.95 | PB | 112PP | ISBN 978 1 78775 865 0 | EISBN 978 1 78775 866 7

Facilitating the healthy management of stress is crucial for social, psychological and emotional wellbeing and resilience in children. This book provides varied and straightforward activities for teachers, parents and therapists to creatively engage with children and help them manage stress. It allows space for children to explore stress, identify some of their worries and build skills and strategies that will help them recognize normal signs of stress and how to respond to these appropriately. It also explore the potential benefits of positive stress, allowing children to have a healthy relationship with difficult feelings.

The accompanying ebook *Using Imagination, Mindful Play and Creative Thinking to Support Wellbeing and Resilience in Children* describes the theory behind this approach and gives examples and guidance for using the activities.

## USING IMAGINATION, MINDFUL PLAY AND CREATIVE THINKING TO SUPPORT WELLBEING AND RESILIENCE IN CHILDREN

*Deborah M. Plummer*

£14.99 | $19.95 | EBOOK | 179PP
| EISBN 978 1 78775 867 4

Forms part of the *Helping Children to Improve Wellbeing and Resilience* series

Using a model of 'mindfulness play' to help children to achieve wellbeing, this book encourages children to build awareness of their inner and outer worlds. This multidimensional approach, designed and developed by an experienced speech and language therapist, centres on the importance of play activities to build psychological, emotional and social wellbeing and looks into the pivotal role adults play in supporting a child's self-esteem. By promoting the growth of self-esteem in different areas of a child's life, the book shows how adults help children to establish a firm basis of wellbeing from which they can flourish.

The accompanying activity booklets that demonstrate the practical application of this approach are:

- *Helping Children to Manage Transitions*
- *Helping Children to Manage Stress*
- *Helping Children to Manage Friendships*
- *Helping Children to Manage Anger*
- *Helping Children to Build Self-Confidence*
- *Helping Children to Build Communication Skills*

The strategies in this ebook guide show how imagination, mindfulness and creativity can enhance our daily interactions with children, and the activity books encourage children to build life skills through structured experiences and through experimenting with different ways of thinking and 'being'.